Become a Tree of LIFE

What really happened in the Garden of Eden

Charles A. West

PivotPointPublishing.com

Become a Tree of Life
Published by:
Pivot Point Publishing
1006 W. Taft STE 166
Sapulpa, OK 74066
PivotPointPublishing.com
ISBN 978-0-615-61655-1

Revised Edition May, 2012

Book production by:
Silver Lining Creative
A Division of Pivot Point Publishing
www.silverliningcreative.com

Printed in the United States of America.

Prelude

This teaching is so different from traditional teachings about the Garden of Eden and what took place there. I would like to assure you, it will in no way go against sound Bible doctrine. In fact, it will strengthen it.

When we enter the Garden of Eden, we will see many things that have been hidden in the Scriptures as the Holy Spirit unveils them for us. You may be thrilled or you may at first be alarmed.

A special thanks to my beautiful wife Marty.
Without her encouragement, help and patience,
this message might have never been completed.

I would also like to thank my best friend, Loyd Umber,
for putting up with me while I was writing this book,
and for his input.

I also want to give a special thank you to Pastor
Orlando Juarez, The Bridge Church, Bixby, Oklahoma,
for his encouragement to complete this book.

Table of Contents

Preface

It is evident we are living in a time when the Holy Spirit is illuminating all the Scriptures that have been hidden for the end time generation; Scriptures concerning end time events, and Scriptures that will be used for the end time harvest.

This message shines a great light on Jesus Christ as the Messiah, the Lord and Savior to all the people on the Earth. I believe this message could be used like a giant combine to help bring in the end time harvest.

– By Charles A. (Chuck) West

Introduction

A few weeks after I received Jesus as my Lord and Savior, I saw a friend's car parked at a bar. John was a young man around 30 years old. He had already undergone liver surgery because of excessive drinking. I was compelled to stop and tell him about Jesus.

I went in and said, "John, you need to accept Jesus Christ as your Lord and Savior." He asked, "Why should I?" I was caught off guard, as I was a baby Christian myself. I did not know what to say at first. Then I heard myself saying, "Because of what happened in the Garden of Eden."

He then asked, "Well, what happened?" I said, "Satan possessed a snake's body and told Eve if she ate from the Tree of the Knowledge of Good and Evil, she would be like God, knowing good and evil. He said, "Stop right there! I have heard that fairy tale before, and I don't want you to waste any more of my time with anything so stupid."

As I headed home, I had never felt so put down or rejected. I was praying as I drove, and I finally said, "Father, what I told John about the Garden of Eden sounds like a fairy tale to me also, but I choose to believe your Word."

Then I heard that small, still voice in my heart say, "Son, what you told him is a fairy tale, and it's been taught that way since Moses' time." I then prayed and asked the Father to please show me what really happened in the Garden of Eden.

A few years later, I enrolled in Victory Bible Institute, Tulsa, Oklahoma. After I graduated, I continued to study the Word of God and to listen to my favorite Bible teachers. I continued to attend church regularly, and I also attended Christ College.

One Sunday, after an evening service, the speaker said, "If you're willing to do whatever it takes for Jesus, come to the front so I can pray for you." I immediately went to the front for prayer. Later, when I went to bed, I could not go to sleep. I tossed and turned for a couple of hours. I finally said, "Lord, are you trying to tell me something?"

I heard that small, still voice in my heart say, "Yes, I want to tell you what happened in the Garden of Eden. Get pen and paper." I went to the kitchen with pen and paper and immediately started writing as the Lord spoke.

When it was finished, I said, "Lord, in the morning I will start sharing this with everyone I know." But the Lord said, "No, you cannot share this with anyone until you have the Scriptures to back it up."

I thought, *when I get up in the morning, I will look up the scriptures quickly and then start sharing this message.* It didn't work out that way. I couldn't find all the Scriptures I needed to share this message. As I continued to go to church and study the Scriptures, the Scriptures I needed started falling in place, to a point where I feel a release in my heart to share this message.

As you hear this message, you will hear some things differently than you have heard them before, but they will not in any way go against the sound doctrine you know. So please keep an open heart. I believe these little golden nuggets will bless you and you will have a higher understanding of the Word of God and its purpose than you've ever had before.

Chapter 1
Keys to Hidden Secrets

But their minds were blinded: for until this day remaineth the same vail untaken away in the reading of the old testament; which vail is done away in Christ.

But even unto this day, when Moses is read, the vail is upon their heart.

Nevertheless when it [one] shall turn to the Lord, the vail shall be taken away.

2 Corinthians 3:14-16

When I read Second Corinthians 3:14-16, I realize the account of what happened in the Garden of Eden was not clearly understood, even in Moses' day. Yet we are still teaching the Genesis account of what happened in the Garden of Eden the same way it was taught in Moses' day.

Here are six keys that will help us see what really happened in the Garden of Eden.

1. The Scriptures are God's Word hidden in men's words. Not hidden *from* us but hidden *for* those who have received Jesus as their Lord and Savior.

2. All Scriptures must harmonize, Old Testament with New Testament.

3. Regarding Bible composites — Old Testament compared to the New Testament — we know that composite drawings are pictures painted from words. When Scriptures in the Old Testament paint the same picture as Scriptures in the New Testament, you could call this a Bible composite. This is probably one of the best ways to check for sound doctrine.

4. Make Scriptural comparisons between the first Adam and the last Adam – Jesus.

5. God's will and purpose for mankind has never changed.

6. Many of the major events and covenants recorded in the Scriptures happened so that Genesis 3:15 would come to pass.

Chapter 2
A Living Soul

And God said, Let us make man in our image, after our likeness: and let them have dominion over the fish of the sea, and over the fowl of the air, and over the cattle, and over all the earth, and over every creeping thing that creepeth upon the earth.

So God created man in his own image, in the image of God created he him; male and female created he them.

Genesis 1:26-27

These Scriptures let us know we are created like God. Man is a spiritual being, so much like God that he can be filled with the Spirit of God. He had the nature of God, he was an eternal being. He was created to be God's companion throughout eternity.

And the LORD God formed man of the dust of the ground, and breathed into his nostrils the breath of life; and man became a living soul.

Genesis 2:7

I'm not going to expound on the subject of man becoming a living soul, but I would like to say this: man as a living soul has reasoning faculties, a free will, and the ability to choose his own destiny. Man has the ability to choose to serve God or not to serve God. God wants a family that will choose Him to be their Father.

Chapter 3
Natural Trees and Supernatural Trees

And the LORD God planted a garden eastward in Eden; and there he put the man whom he had formed.

And out of the ground made the LORD God to grow every tree that is pleasant to the sight, and good for food; the tree of life also in the midst of the garden, and the tree of knowledge of good and evil.

Genesis 2:8-9

The trees that grew out of the ground were natural trees, much like the trees we have today.

There were also some supernatural trees in the garden. These trees were called the Tree of Life and the Tree of The Knowledge of Good and Evil. These trees did not grow out of the ground. They were in the midst of the garden. If you look up the word "midst" used here in *Strong's Concordance*, it says "among." *Webster's Dictionary* says "the interior or central part or place." In other words, not stationary.

I knew the names Adam had given every creature were descriptive and wondered if the word "tree" had a descriptive meaning. Then I heard a small, still voice in my heart say, "Look up the word *tree* in an encyclopedia." A neighbor happened to have a new set of *World Book Encyclopedias*.

The first paragraph said, "A tree has three main parts, the roots, the trunk and the branches, and the leaves." I realized how precious this is — a tree has three main parts and these three are one. Then the Holy Ghost quickened a Scripture to me.

First John 5:7 says,

For there are three that bear record in heaven, the Father, the Word, and the Holy Ghost: and these three are one.

All of a sudden it was so clear; all life comes from the Father, the Word, and the Holy Ghost. They are the Tree of Life. The natural trees produced the natural food. The food from the Tree of Life was then, and is today, the Word of God.

In Matthew 4:4 we read,

But he [Jesus] answered and said, It is written, Man shall not live by bread alone, but by every word that proceedeth out of the mouth of God.

Satan always offers a counterfeit for all the good things the Father has for man. Satan is the Tree of the Knowledge of Good and Evil. The food Satan had to offer from the Tree of the Knowledge of Good and Evil was then, and is today, false doctrine.

From this point on, as you read this book and see the term "Tree of Life," do not picture in your mind a tree. The name "Tree of Life" is simply another name for the Father God. The term "Tree of the Knowledge of Good and Evil" is simply another name for Satan, who is also called the serpent, the dragon, and the devil.

God did not create a fruit tree growing out of the ground to tempt Adam with evil. James 1:3 says, *"Let no man say when he is tempted, I am tempted of God, for God cannot be tempted with evil, neither tempteth he any man."* When God commanded Adam not to eat from the Tree of the Knowledge of Good and Evil, He knew that Satan went to and fro on the earth and that he would be in the midst of the Garden of Eden on occasion.

> Now there was a day when the sons of God came to present themselves before the LORD, and Satan came also among them.
>
> And the LORD said unto Satan, Whence comest thou? Then Satan answered the LORD, and said, From going to and fro in the earth, and from walking up and down in it. [Notice God will talk to Satan.]

Job 1: 6-7

Isaiah 14:12-14 tells us,

> How art thou fallen from heaven, O Lucifer, son of the morning! how art thou cut down to the ground, which didst weaken the nations!
>
> For thou hast said in thine heart, I will ascend into heaven, I will exalt my throne above the stars of God: I will sit also upon the mount of the congregation, in the sides of the north:
>
> I will ascend above the heights of the clouds; I will be like the most High.

These Scriptures let us know Satan's name was Lucifer until he fell from heaven.

> Thou wast perfect in thy ways from the day that thou wast created, till iniquity was found in thee.

Ezekiel 28:15,

This Scripture lets us know God created Lucifer perfect until iniquity was found in him. Please read Ezekiel 28:11-18.

Remember, God did not create Satan to tempt Adam with evil, but God did warn Adam that Satan would try to feed him false doctrine and commanded the man

7

not to eat. This meant, "Don't believe or accept what he says."

First Peter 5:8 says,

Be sober, be vigilant; because your adversary the devil, as a roaring lion, walketh about, seeking whom he may devour:

This Scripture lets us know things have not changed much.

Chapter 4
Adam Was Alone

Aｎd the LORD God commanded the man, saying, Of every tree of the garden thou mayest freely eat:

But of the tree of the knowledge of good and evil, thou shalt not eat of it: for in the day that thou eatest thereof thou shalt surely die.

Genesis 2:16-17

Man was commanded to eat of every tree in the Garden of Eden. This included the Tree of Life, but of the Tree of the Knowledge of Good and Evil, he was commanded not to eat. The commandment starts at the first of verse 16.

It is evident from the Scriptures that God had been teaching and instructing Adam, and that Adam was extremely intelligent. Adam knew how much natural food he should eat to be healthy. But as a living soul, God left the choice up to him. Adam also knew how much time he should spend feeding on God's Word, so he would know to refuse the evil and choose the good. (This is a key phrase; keep it in your remembrance.) Again, the choice was Adam's.

Concerning the Tree of the Knowledge of Good and Evil, God gave Adam no choice. God said, "*Thou shall not eat of it: for in the day that thou eatest thereof thou shalt surely die.*" Of course, as a living soul, Adam had the ability to break God's commandment.

And the LORD God said, It is not good that the man should be alone; I will make him an help meet for him.

Genesis 2:18

After an allotted amount of time had passed, this is an interesting comment God makes about Adam, after he has been commanded to eat from the natural trees, (natural food) and from the Tree of Life (God's Word).

In verse 18 God said, "*It is not good that the man should be alone.*" Did God make a mistake and create Adam alone? Genesis chapter one tells us that everything God created was good. It's evident Adam was not feeding on God's Word; he was not pleasing the Father God. Adam is quickly approaching a time when he will be held accountable for having the knowledge of God's Word and how to operate in the authority of it.

Let's make a comparison. The last Adam came to earth to destroy the works of the devil by fulfilling what the first Adam failed to do. First Corinthians 15, 45-47 lets us know that Jesus was the last Adam.

In Isaiah 7:14-15 we read,

Therefore the Lord himself shall give you a sign; Behold, a virgin shall conceive, and bear a son, and shall call his name Immanuel. [Literally, this means "God with us."]

Butter and honey shall he eat, that he may know to refuse the evil, and choose the good.

Jesus had laid down His glory, and like a man when He was born on the earth, He did not know right from wrong. The butter and honey represent God's Word. This harmonizes with the Scriptures, Old Testament and New. God's Word is the only food that teaches us the difference between good and evil.

Then said Jesus unto them, When ye have lifted up the Son of man, then shall ye know that I am he, and that I do nothing of myself; but as my Father hath taught me, I speak these things.

And he that sent me is with me: the Father hath not left me alone; for I do always those things that please him.

John 8:28-29

Jesus, the last Adam, was not alone because He was pleasing the Father, and He was waxing strong in the Spirit as he fed from the Tree of Life (God's Word).

Based on the Scriptures, it's evident that Adam wasn't pleasing the Father. God wanted Adam to make the choice to feed from the Tree of Life until he knew to refuse the evil and choose the good. Then the Father would fill Adam with the Holy Spirit and he would never be alone. Then God would make the woman for Adam, and Adam would take the woman to the Tree of Life to feed on God's Word until she knew to choose the good and refuse the evil. Then God would have blessed them and said be fruitful and multiply and replenish the earth. They would then take their children to feed from the Tree of Life. This would be a continuous cycle.

God's priorities for man have never changed. Men and women should receive the new birth and have a personal, intimate relationship with God the Father as they feed on God's Word, until they know to refuse the evil and choose the good. Then if they choose to get married and have children, they should see that their children repeat the same cycle.

Chapter 5
An Angel of Light

And I saw an angel come down from heaven, having the key of the bottomless pit and a great chain in his hand.

And he laid hold on the dragon, that old serpent, which is the Devil, and Satan, and bound him a thousand years,

Revelation 20:1-2

From this scripture we learn the term serpent used in Genesis 3:1-7 is one of the names used to describe Satan. Second Corinthians 11: 3 says,

But I fear, lest by any means, as the serpent beguiled Eve through his subtilty, so your minds should be corrupted from the simplicity that is in Christ.

If you look up the word "serpent" used here in *Strong's Concordance*, it says, "a snake, a figure of speech [as a type of sly cunning] an artful malicious person, especially Satan."

Second Corinthians 11:14 tells us,

And no marvel; for Satan himself is transformed into an angel of light. [He transforms himself.]

The definition of the word "transformed" from the *Strong's Concordance* is to "transfigure or disguise." No other body needed. If Satan can disguise himself to

13

look like a beautiful angel of light, full of wisdom, why would he get in a snake's body to talk to the woman?

Moses wrote what the Lord inspired him to write when he wrote the book of Genesis. He probably didn't have any idea what really happened in the Garden of Eden. His generation didn't need to know. When one turns to the Lord, the veil is done away in Christ. Because of this, it is evident the end time generation does need to know.

Paul knew what happened by revelations from Jesus Christ. In 2 Corinthians 11:3-4 and 11:12-15, Paul says in verses 3-4,

> **But I fear, lest by any means, as the serpent beguiled Eve through his subtilty, so your minds should be corrupted from the simplicity that is in Christ.**
>
> **For if he that cometh preacheth another Jesus, whom we have not preached, or if ye receive another spirit, which ye have not received, or another gospel, which ye have not accepted, ye might well bear with him.**

In verses 12-15 Paul says,

> **But what I do, that I will do, that I may cut off occasion from them which desire occasion; that wherein they glory, they may be found even as we.**
>
> **For such are false apostles, deceitful workers, transforming themselves into the apostles of Christ.**
>
> **And no marvel; for Satan himself is transformed into an angel of light.**
>
> **Therefore it is no great thing if his ministers also be transformed as the ministers of righteousness; whose end shall be according to their works.**

Paul is telling us Eve received false doctrine from Satan, who is called the Tree of the Knowledge of Good and Evil. Paul is concerned that as the devil was transformed into an angel of light and deceived Eve with false doctrine, the Corinthians will be deceived with false doctrine by these false apostles of Christ, as they transform themselves to look like ministers of righteousness.

When Paul says Satan is transformed into an angel of light, the word "light" here means illumination, mental illumination, and full of knowledge or information, something to be desired to make one wise.

Chapter 6
Receiving False Doctrine

A nd when the woman saw that the tree was good for food, and that it was pleasant to the eyes, and a tree to be desired to make one wise, she took of the fruit thereof, and did eat, and gave also unto her husband with her; [when he was with her] and he did eat.

Genesis 3:6

Strong's Concordance says the Hebrew word used here for *took* is number 3947, *laqach*. The definition is "to take [in the widest variety of applications]." It is a way of receiving physically. Taken from laqach 3948, leqach is another application of 3947. Its definition says "Something received [mentally], instruction [whether on the part of the teacher or hearer]; also inveiglement, doctrine, learning, fair speech."

When the original Hebrew manuscripts were being translated into Elizabethan English, if a word had a variety of applications, the main priority was to use the word that best fits the context of what was being said. Without proper discernment, the wrong word was sometimes used.

Think back on 2 Corinthians 11:3-15. Here Paul lets us know that Eve received false doctrine — that's what she took. This is a perfect Bible composite of what she took in Genesis 3:6. The translators simply used the wrong application for the word "took."

17

Genesis 3:6 says, *"She took of the fruit thereof, and did eat."* This word "eat" is the same word "eat" used in Jeremiah 15:16.

Thy words were found, and I did eat them; and thy word was unto me the joy and rejoicing of mine heart: for I am called by thy name, O LORD God of hosts.

Eve had eaten false doctrine and had received it into her heart. This makes an exact Bible composite of what Paul said could happen in 2 Corinthians 11.

Chapter 7
Spiritual Death

And the LORD God said unto the woman, What is this that thou hast done? And the woman said, The serpent beguiled me, and I did eat.

Genesis 3:13

This lets us know that the woman was deceived. It's evident that Adam wasn't with Eve when she received false doctrine from Satan. Eve had hearkened to the voice of Satan and had received false doctrine.

In Genesis 3:17 we read,

And unto Adam he said, Because thou hast hearkened unto the voice of thy wife, and hast eaten of the tree, of which I commanded thee, saying, Thou shalt not eat of it: cursed is the ground for thy sake; in sorrow shalt thou eat of it all the days of thy life;

When Adam was with Eve, he harkened to her voice and ate her words. This means he had received false doctrine into his heart. He had actually eaten from The Tree of the Knowledge of Good and Evil.

In verse 13 Eve said, *"The serpent beguiled me and I did eat."* In verse 12 Adam said, *"She gave me of the tree and I did eat."* Eve had become a Tree of the Knowledge of Good and Evil. She had become a carrier of false doctrine.

For Adam was first formed, then Eve.

And Adam was not deceived, but the woman being deceived was in the transgression.

1Timothy 2:13-14

The word "transgression" used here according to Strong's Concordance means to "violate a command." Eve violated God's command because she was deceived. Why did Adam break God's command?

Hosea 4:6 says,

My people are destroyed for lack of knowledge: because thou hast rejected knowledge, I will also reject thee, that thou shalt be no priest to me: seeing thou hast forgotten the law of thy God, I will also forget thy children.

Hosea 6:6-7 goes on to say,

For I delight in loyalty rather than sacrifice, And in the knowledge of God rather than burnt offerings.

But like Adam they have transgressed the covenant; There they have dealt treacherously against Me. (NASV)

The definition of the word "treacherously" used in verse seven, according to the *New World Dictionary*, is as follows: "betrayal of trust, faith, or allegiance; perfidy, disloyalty or treason." Adam had committed treason when he gave up the dominion over the earth to God's arch enemy. This was a treacherous act.

Things are much the same today as they were then. If Adam and Eve had fed from the Tree of Life (God's Word) until they knew to choose the good and refuse the evil, they wouldn't have broken the covenant they made with God. Ignorance is no excuse. There comes a time in everyone's life when you become accountable to know God's Word and how to use it.

This time came in the last Adam's life right after He was baptized by John the Baptist and filled with the Holy Ghost. Read Matthew 4: 1-11. The tempter came to Jesus and tried to feed Him false doctrine. Jesus, the last Adam, refused to eat false doctrine. Jesus spoke the written Word of God to Satan until the devil left. The last Adam had chosen the good and refused the evil, and He wasn't alone.

And the LORD God said, Behold, the man is become as one of us, to know good and evil: and now, lest he put forth his hand, and take also of the tree of life, and eat, and live for ever:

Therefore the LORD God sent him forth from the garden of Eden, to till the ground from whence he was taken.

So he drove out the man; and he placed at the east of the garden of Eden Cherubims, and a flaming sword which turned every way, to keep [protect] the way of the tree of life [the Way].

Genesis 3:22-24

Man was separated from the Tree of Life. Of course this means he was separated from God (the Trinity). Man died spiritually at this time. Separation from God is spiritual death. Man was lost, without hope, except for what the Lord God had prophesied in Genesis 3:15.

Let's look further to see what Adam and Eve had lost. Genesis 3:22 tells us, *"And the Lord God said, Behold the man is become as one of us, to know good and evil."* To whom does "one of us" refer to here? To the ones present with the Lord God in Genesis chapter three — Adam, Eve, and Satan. This lets us know it was Satan the Lord God spoke to when He said, *"Behold the man is become as one of us, to know good and evil."*

The Amplified Bible is the only translation I can find that takes the liberty to insinuate the Scriptures were referring to the Father, the Son, and the Holy Spirit. This does not harmonize with God's Word. Remember, the word "amplified" means something was added to the original manuscripts to help us understand the Scriptures. When words were added, some mistakes were made when the translators lacked illumination of the Scriptures.

The Scriptures let us know the Father wants us to be as much like Him as possible. We are spiritual beings, and we have His nature. We're created in His image and after His likeness. We can receive His Spirit. We also have the mind of Christ.

We're told in Ephesians 5:1, *"Be ye followers of God, as dear children."* *Strong's Concordance* says the term "followers of God" means imitators of God. This is God's will for us — to be like Him, to be like Jesus, and to know to refuse the evil and choose the good.

In Genesis 3:22 the Scripture says, *"Behold the man is become as one of us to know good and evil."* The definition of the word "know" used here from the Strong's Concordance is "endued with." *The New World Dictionary* says the word "endue" means "to endow [with qualities, talents, etc.]."

This lets us know that Adam and Eve had been recreated; they had God's love nature, and they had been endowed with Satan's evil nature. Satan had become a joint creator of man with God. Satan's plan was to become a partner with God, and a joint ruler with God over the man and the earth.

Man had become a hybrid. *The New World Dictionary's* definition of hybrid is, "The offspring produced by crossing two individuals of unlike genetic constitution."

If God left man in this condition, he would be able to feed from the Tree of Life (God's Word) and live forever as God and Satan's joint creation.

Adam had broken the covenant he had made with God. So God had a legal right to set aside the covenant He had made with Adam.

Genesis 3:22 shows us the Lord God separated man from the Tree of Life, the Father, the Word, and the Holy Spirit. This lets us know that the Lord God removed His nature, His Spirit, and His Word from Adam and Eve. This condition is called *spiritual death*.

At this time man only had the nature of his new father, the devil. Man was now led by his five physical senses and false doctrine from his new father.

John 8:44 tells us the condition Adam and Eve were in. Jesus speaks to the scribes and Pharisees, the most religious people of the time, and says, *"Ye are of your father the devil, and the lusts of your father ye will do."* This shows us man's condition was hopeless except for God's plan in Genesis 3:15 to provide a way back to the Tree of Life.

This harmonizes with Ezekiel 36: 26-27, which says,

A new heart also will I give you, and a new spirit will I put within you: and I will take away the stony heart out of your flesh, and I will give you an heart of flesh.

And I will put my spirit within you, and cause you to walk in my statutes, and ye shall keep my judgments, and do them.

This is a prophecy of the new birth. This gives man back what he lost in the Garden of Eden.

Chapter 8
God's Plan to Redeem Man*

And I will put enmity between thee and the woman, and between thy seed and her seed; it shall bruise thy head, and thou shalt bruise his heel.

Genesis 3:15

1. *"And I will put enmity between thee and the woman."* That is, there will be hatred and hostility between Satan and the woman. This is proven by woman's history. She has been bought and sold as common chattel. Only where Christianity has reached the hearts of a country, have women ever received their place in society.

2. *"And I will put enmity between thy seed and her seed."* Satan's seed is the unregenerate human race and woman's seed is Christ. Christ was hunted from His babyhood by Satan's seed, until finally they nailed Him to the cross. And from the resurrection of Jesus until this day, the Church has been the subject of the bitterest persecutions and hatred and hostility of the world.

3. The seed of the woman is a prophecy that a woman shall give birth to a child independent of natural generation. A child is always called the *seed of man*. This is a prophecy of the virgin birth.

4. It says, *"he shall bruise thy head,"* that is the head of Satan. In all oriental languages, the term "bruise thy head" means *breaking the lordship of the ruler.*

5. The heel is the Church in its earth walk. The long ages of persecution of the Church by the seed of Satan are a matter of history.

Satan realized the fact that a Redeemer was coming through humanity who would break his dominion over man. He therefore seeks to destroy the plan of Father God. The working of Satan to destroy the purpose of God followed these lines:

1. Destroy the knowledge of God and His will on the earth.

2. Destroy a righteous line in humanity so man would have no way back to the Tree of Life.

3. Destroying God's covenant with Abraham by corrupting Abraham's seed, so the covenant wouldn't be valid.

---

* Excerpt from E.W. Kenyon's book, *The Bible in the Light of Our Redemption*

Chapter 9
The Way

So he drove out the man; and he placed at the east of the garden of Eden Cherubims, and a flaming sword which turned every way, to keep [guard] the way of the tree of life.

Genesis 3:24

God immediately took the necessary steps to see that His plan to break the power of sin and redeem man is carried out. Notice it says to "keep [guard] the way," not the Tree.

Vines Expository Dictionary says, "The first reference to the cherubim is in Genesis 3:24, which should read, 'At the east of the Garden of Eden, He caused to dwell in a tabernacle the cherubim and the flaming sword, which turned itself to keep the way of the Tree of Life.' This was not simply to keep fallen human beings out; the presence of the cherubim suggests that redeemed men, restored to God on God's conditions, would have access to the Tree of Life."

Ephesians 6:17 states,

And take the helmet of salvation, and the sword of the Spirit, which is the word of God:

Cherubims are mighty angels, and the flaming sword represents the authority to operate in the power of God's Word. God sent cherubims with the authority to use His Word to protect the way of the Tree of Life, man's way back to Father God, to see that Genesis 3:15 was carried out. To be legal, God's plan in Genesis 3:15 would have to correspond with the allotted time God had given Adam the dominion over the earth. This dominion had been handed over to Satan.

From this time until Genesis 3:15 is fulfilled, most major events and covenants that are recorded in the Bible are directly or indirectly related to Genesis 3:15, to see that God's plan (Word) is carried out.

I will worship toward thy holy temple, and praise thy name for thy loving kindness and for thy truth: for thou hast magnified thy word above all thy name.

Psalm 138:2

God's Word is so important to Him, He will do whatever it takes to see that it is fulfilled. We can always count on it.

In Genesis chapter 15, God tells us of a blood covenant He cut with Abraham. In Genesis chapter 22, God tells Abraham to offer his only son Isaac for a burnt offering. Abraham took Isaac to the mountain, and when he raised the knife to kill him, the angel of the Lord stopped him. This act ratified the covenant. This gave the Father God the legal right to use Abraham's seed to provide a body for Jesus, at the appointed time.

Wherefore when he [Jesus] cometh into the world, he saith, Sacrifice and offering thou wouldest not, but a body hast thou prepared me: **Hebrews 10:5**

It also gave God the Father the right to offer Jesus Christ, His Son, to redeem mankind when the time was right.

Now to Abraham and his seed were the promises made. He saith not, And to seeds, as of many; but as of one, And to thy seed, which is Christ.

Galatians 3:16

Jesus Christ would be man's way back to the Father God (The Trinity).

Chapter 10
Bible Composites

L et's look at a couple of Bible composites that shine light on this teaching.

1. Genesis 3:22 says, *"And the Lord God said, Behold the man has become as one of us, to know good and evil: and now lest he put forth his hand, and take also of the Tree of Life and eat, and live forever."* It is evident the food offered from the Tree of Life would make you live forever. Remember, I said the food offered from the Tree of Life was the Word of God.

2. Jesus says in John 6:51, *"I am the living bread which came down from heaven: if any man eats of this bread, he shall live forever: and the bread that I will give is my flesh, which I will give for the life of the world."* This bread is the Word of God. Notice, talking about Jesus in John 1:14, it says, *"And the Word was made flesh, and dwelt among us."* Jesus is talking about eating God's Word and receiving Him as your Lord and Savior. Genesis 3:22 and John 6:51 are Bible composites, Old Testament to the New Testament.

3. Genesis 3:24 tells us, *"So he drove out the man: and he placed at the east of the Garden of Eden Cherubims, and a flaming sword which turned every way, to keep the way of the*

Tree of Life." Remember, I said the way of the Tree of Life was the way back to the Father.

4. John 14:6 says, *"Jesus saith unto him, I am the way, the truth, and the life: no man cometh to the Father but by me."* The "way" in Genesis 3:24 and the "way" in John 14:6 are the only way to the Father. The way is Jesus Christ. Genesis 3:24 and John 14:6 are Bible composites Old Testament to the New Testament. Please read Romans chapter 5.

Chapter 11
Become a New Creation

Would you like to become a child of God and be able to feed from the Tree of Life, (The Father, Son and Holy Spirit), be able to feed on God's Word, and to understand the hidden treasures and blessings God has for His children?

If the answer is yes, turn in your Bible to Romans 10:9-10, which says,

That if thou shalt confess with thy mouth the Lord Jesus, and shalt believe in thine heart that God hath raised him from the dead, thou shalt be saved.

For with the heart man believeth unto righteousness; and with the mouth confession is made unto salvation.

Say this prayer and believe in your heart what you say is true and you will be saved:

Jesus, I ask you to be my Lord. I believe you died for my sins and God has raised you from the dead. I believe you are seated at the right hand of God in heaven. Please come into my heart and be my Lord forever. Amen.

When you say this prayer, a miracle takes place. The Holy Spirit baptizes you into the Body of Christ. Your name is written in the Lamb's Book of Life. You receive God's Spirit and His nature. You have become a member of God's family, with family rights.

These Scriptures will help you see what instantly takes place when you are born again.

For as the body is one, and hath many members, and all the members of that one body, being many, are one body: so also is Christ.

For by one Spirit are we all baptized into one body, whether we be Jews or Gentiles, whether we be bond or free; and have been all made to drink into one Spirit.

For the body is not one member, but many.

1 Corinthians 12:12-14

Not by works of righteousness which we have done, but according to his mercy he saved us, by the washing of regeneration, and renewing of the Holy Ghost;

Which he shed on us abundantly through Jesus Christ our Saviour;

That being justified by his grace, we should be made heirs according to the hope of eternal life.

Titus 3: 5-7

You are now a new creation in Jesus Christ! You can feed from the Tree of Life and understand God's Word.

Chapter 12
Become a Tree of Life

N ow that you can *feed* from the Tree of Life, would you like to *become* a Tree of Life? Proverbs 3: 13-18 in the Amplified Bible says,

, **Happy (blessed, fortunate, enviable) is the man who finds skillful and godly Wisdom, and the man who gets understanding [drawing it forth from God's Word and life's experiences],**

For the gaining of it is better than the gaining of silver, and the profit of it better than fine gold.

Skillful and godly Wisdom is more precious than rubies; and nothing you can wish for is to be compared to her.

Length of days is in her right hand, and in her left hand are riches and honor.

Her ways are highways of pleasantness, and all her paths are peace.

She is a tree of life to those who lay hold on her; and happy (blessed, fortunate, to be envied) is everyone who holds her fast.

These Scriptures let us know when we find skillful and godly wisdom and get understanding, drawing it forth from God's Word, as we feed from the Tree of Life, the Word of God abides in us.

> The fruit of the [uncompromisingly] righteous is a tree of life, and he who is wise captures human lives [for God, as a fisher of men — he gathers and receives them for eternity].
>
> Proverbs 11:30 (AMP)

These Scriptures let us know that after we receive the new birth and eat from the Tree of Life and share God's Word, we have become a tree of life. Not *the* Tree of Life (the Trinity), but *a* tree of life, sharing God's Word.

> For in Him the whole fullness of Deity (the Godhead) continues to dwell in bodily form [giving complete expression of the divine nature].
>
> And you are in Him, made full and having come to fullness of life [in Christ you too are filled with the Godhead — Father, Son and Holy Spirit — and reach full spiritual stature]. And He is the Head of all rule and authority [of every angelic principality and power].
>
> Colossians 2:9-10 (AMP)

This Scripture lets us know that in Jesus we are filled with the fullness of the Godhead bodily. Yes, indeed, we have become a tree of life. Amen.

Conclusion

In closing, in the Scriptures, trees are often used to represent man.

For a good tree bringeth not forth corrupt fruit; neither doth a corrupt tree bring forth good fruit.

For every tree is known by his own fruit. For of thorns men do not gather figs, nor of a bramble bush gather they grapes.

A good man out of the good treasure of his heart bringeth forth that which is good; and an evil man out of the evil treasure of his heart bringeth forth that which is evil: for of the abundance of the heart his mouth speaketh.

Luke 6:43-45

At this time, you could say the *Tree of Life* and the *Tree of the Knowledge of Good and Evil* are family trees. The *Tree of Life* represents God's family, and the *Tree of the Knowledge of Good and Evil* represents Satan's family.

To contact the author:

Email:

atreeoflife@cox.net

PivotPointPublishing.com